THE
HEALTHY DOG
COOKBOOK

THE
HEALTHY DOG
COOKBOOK

A Cookbook of 50 Nutritious & Delicious Recipes Your Dog Will Love

JONNA ANNE
with MARY STRAUS, CANINE NUTRITIONIST
Shawn Messonnier, DVM, Veterinary Consultant

IVY PRESS

This edition was published in the UK in 2016 by
Ivy Press
210 High Street
Lewes
East Sussex BN7 2NS
United Kingdom
www.ivypress.co.uk

First published in 2008

British Library Cataloguing-in-Publication Data
A catalogue record for this book is available from the British Library

ISBN: 978-1-78240-357-9

This book was conceived, designed and produced by
Ivy Press
Creative Director Peter Bridgewater
Publisher Jason Hook
Editorial Director Caroline Earle
Senior Project Editor Stephanie Evans
Art Director Sarah Howerd
Designer Joanna Clinch
Illustrator Joanna Kerr
Photographer Andrew Perris
Consultant Canine Nutritionist Mary Straus
Consultant Veterinarian Dr Shawn Messonnier

This book has been published with the intent to provide accurate and authoritative information in regard to the subject matter within. While every reasonable precaution has been taken in preparation of this book, the author and publisher expressly disclaim responsibility for any errors, omissions or adverse effects arising from the use or application of the information contained herein. The techniques and suggestions are used at the reader's discretion and are not to be considered a substitute for veterinary care. If you suspect a medical problem, consult your veterinarian.

Printed in China

10 9 8 7 6 5 4 3 2 1

Contents

Introduction

Can you imagine how dull it would be to eat the same food every day? There are many reasons to feed your dog home-made meals, not the least of which is the enjoyment they provide.

Many picky feeders become chow hounds when offered fresh, home-cooked food in place of (or added to) plain, commercial dog food. When you make your dog's food yourself, you have complete control over everything you feed, so you don't have to worry about the possibility of adulterated or contaminated ingredients, and you can identify and avoid any foods that cause problems for your dog.

THE LOW-DOWN ON COMMERCIAL FOODS

Many people find that their dogs become healthier as well as happier when fed a home-made diet. Commercial dog foods lose much of their nutritional value during processing, which must then be added back in the form of synthetic vitamins and minerals that cannot replace all the nutrients found in fresh foods. Poor-quality ingredients, artificial colourings, preservatives and other chemicals can lead to allergies and health problems. However, good-quality ready-prepared meals made by reputable manufacturers of natural dog foods can be used in conjunction with home-prepared food.

THE RIGHT DIET

Dry dog foods are often 50 per cent (or more) carbohydrates. Some veterinarians and owners noticed that these diets can increase skin, intestinal and joint inflammation related to allergies and arthritis. Home-made diets, particularly those high in protein and low in carbohydrates, are often easier to digest and provide superior nutrition that can lead to a longer and healthier life.

BACK TO BASICS

Preparing meals for your dog is not hard, but it is vital that it be done correctly and not merely consist of table scraps. Read this section thoroughly before using the recipes if you intend to feed your dog a home-made diet. You can also use these recipes to add fresh foods to your dog's diet, even if you continue to feed commercial foods.

DO WHAT WORKS
Remember that your pet is an individual. One of the benefits of a home-made diet is how easily it can be modified to meet your dog's special needs. Do what works for your dog, but don't limit the menu to just a few favourites.

Canine Nutrition

There are three very important factors
to remember when you feed your dog
a home-made diet: calcium, variety and
balance over time.

VARIETY

**If you want to feed
some commercial dog
food, rotate brands
and protein sources
to provide variety
and better nutrition.
Adding fresh foods
will improve your pet's
diet and make it more
appealing.**

CALCIUM: THE CRUCIAL INGREDIENT

Calcium must be added to any home-made diet to
keep bones healthy and strong. Without the proper
amount of calcium added to the diet, bones will
weaken and eventually break. There is not enough
calcium in any food other than bones to meet your
dog's nutritional needs. Adult dogs need around
800–1,000 mg of calcium added per 450 g (1 lb)
of food. (For puppies, see page 15.) Any form of
calcium can be used, including eggshell, which
should be ground (not just crushed) in a clean
coffee or spice grinder; then add ½ teaspoon of this
ground eggshell per 450 g (1 lb) of food. Bonemeal
can also be used to supply calcium, but because
it contains phosphorus as well, you need to
give a little more than when using
plain calcium. Add an amount
of bonemeal that provides
around 1,200 mg of
calcium per 450 g
(1 lb) of food.

Calcium can be added at feeding time, or to the whole recipe when the food is prepared, as it's not affected by storage. Another option is to use one of the vitamin-mineral mixtures specifically designed to balance out a home-made diet, including supplying the proper amount of calcium. Make sure that the mix is guaranteed to meet FEDIAF – the European Pet Food Industry Federation – nutritional guidelines when used according to instructions.

Know Your Pet

Introduce different meats (such as beef, lamb, pork, chicken and turkey) gradually to see if any do not agree with your dog. Other meats such as buffalo, venison or duck (see pages 48, 52 and 116) can be tried if you suspect food allergies, but reserve at least one or two for future use in case a novel protein is needed.

A HEALTHY VARIETY

Feed a wide variety of foods to help meet all of your dog's nutritional needs. It's best to feed different types of meat as well as other foods, including fish, offal, eggs and dairy. Liver is especially rich in nutrients and should make up around 5 per cent of the total diet, or around 28 g (1 oz) of liver per 450 g (1 lb) of other meats. Feed small amounts frequently – large amounts at one time can lead to loose stools. Heart is another organ meat that's good to feed. Healthy leftovers – foods you would eat yourself – are a fine addition to the diet. You can add an egg or a small amount of liver to any meal, or garnish with a spoonful of yogurt or cottage cheese for extra flavour and nutrition.

GETTING THE RIGHT BALANCE

It is not necessary for every meal to be nutritionally complete as long as the diet you feed is balanced over time. Think about your own diet – and what you feed your children – providing different foods at each meal that together create a balanced diet.

Protein, Fat & Carbohydrates

Dogs evolved as carnivores and thrive on high-protein diets for which bulk, in the form of carbohydrates, is no substitute.

Protein provides many benefits: it contributes to a healthy skin and coat, aids wound healing, supports the immune system and the nervous system and promotes lean muscle over fat. Increasing the amount of high-quality protein in the diet can help both to calm hyperactive dogs and to energize sluggish and overweight pets.

THE RIGHT SOURCE OF CALORIES

Animal protein is especially important for dogs. Plant proteins are incomplete and harder for carnivores to digest. Home-made diets should be at least half animal products (meat, eggs, fish and dairy) and no more than half plant products (grains, vegetables, pulses).

Fat is also good for dogs, particularly animal fat rather than vegetable oils (cholesterol is generally not a problem for dogs). Fat is used for energy, so it's especially important for very active dogs that

SATURATED FAT
Unlike people, dogs don't have to worry about clogged arteries, so saturated fats are not a concern.

have trouble maintaining their weight. Less active and overweight pets need less fat, but do not feed a very low-fat diet unless your dog has a fat intolerance. Too little fat leads to skin conditions and a dull, lifeless coat. It also leaves the dog feeling hungry all the time, which can introduce behavioural problems.

CARBOHYDRATES & CANINES

Carbohydrates, which come from plants such as grains, vegetables and fruits, offer an inexpensive source of calories for your dog but have less nutritional value than foods from animal sources. Carbohydrates can also contribute to weight gain. Recent studies show that traditional high-carb, low-fat diets are not the best choice for weight loss. Instead, feed a high-protein, moderate-fat, low-carb diet if a dog is overweight, and increase exercise gradually.

Many health problems in dogs may be linked to high-carb diets. If your dog suffers from allergies, arthritis, seizures, urine leaking, chronic ear infections or digestive disorders, omit grains and starchy carbs from the diet for a while to see if your dog's condition improves.

Some dogs have a gluten intolerance and cannot handle certain grains. Gluten-free substitutes for regular flour include gram, almond, potato, tapioca, arrowroot, soya, rice, amaranth, millet and quinoa flour. Buckwheat, rye, oat and barley flours are not gluten-free but can be used for dogs that have problems with wheat.

Puppies & Seniors

Both puppies and seniors require more protein than younger adult dogs. Newer studies have proved that high-protein diets do not cause orthopedic problems in puppies, nor do they lead to kidney disease in older dogs. With the exception of a very few specific health problems, feeding a diet that is high in protein offers benefits to every dog.

Food Preparation

Once you have done some shopping and are ready to get started, preparation is easy and satisfying, knowing that you are doing your best for your pet.

Food can be prepared in large batches and frozen in portions to make the process easier. Do not leave uneaten food out once it has been served or it will spoil. Store leftovers in the fridge. Your dog may prefer that refrigerated food be allowed to come to room temperature before feeding.

COOKED OR RAW?

Some nutrients are lost through cooking, especially for a long time at high temperatures. Meats are best cooked lightly at low temperatures to preserve nutritional value. Eggs can be soft-cooked, hard-boiled or scrambled. Meat and eggs can also be fed raw, if you are comfortable doing so. While it is possible for dogs to be affected by bacteria found in raw food, it is unusual, especially for healthy dogs. If your dog is delicate, ill or has a compromised immune system, it's always best to cook the meat.

Off the Bone

It is essential that all bones be removed from poultry. Cooked bones will break into jagged splinters that can pierce your dog's digestive system, causing serious injury. Remove fish bones for the same reason (tinned fish bones are soft and safe to feed).

The way you cook the food is important. Boiling in particular, and steaming to a lesser extent, leaches out minerals, though some are returned if you feed the cooking water. Boiling removes fat, which can be helpful if your dog has a fat intolerance but is otherwise unnecessary. Steaming is a good way to cook vegetables; again include the water. Add leftover meat drippings, gravy, soups, sauces or chicken carcass (remove bones before feeding) during cooking to make a savoury stock.

FRUIT & VEG
Most fruits can be fed raw, though it's best to choose ripe ones, which are easier to digest. Vegetables are best fed cooked or puréed to break down the cell walls. While not harmful, whole raw vegetables provide little nutritional value. Grains, pulses and starchy vegetables such as potatoes, sweet potatoes and winter squashes must be fully cooked in order to be digestible.

NATURAL FLAVOURINGS
Herbs and spices are fine to add if your dog likes them (and many do, especially aniseed).

GARLIC & ONION
These two alliums have different properties. Onions, cooked or raw, should not be fed to dogs, as they cause anaemia, though very small amounts in leftovers should not be a problem. Unless your vet advises against it for your particular breed of dog, a little crushed garlic is fine – no more than 1 small clove per 9 kg (20 lb) of body weight daily.

Off the Vine

Never feed your pet grapes, raisins or sultanas, as these fruits have been linked to kidney failure in dogs. For the same reason, avoid grape juice too.

Amount to Feed

Each dog is an individual, and the amount of food needed will vary considerably, depending on activity level and metabolism, as well as the amount of fat in the diet.

PORTION SIZE

Portion sizes for each recipe are based on the number of calories needed twice a day by a moderately active adult dog (puppies eat more). For recipes that make a number of portions, for convenience in dividing them you could use a scoop or mug that holds 240 ml (8 fl oz) of water – this is approximately one portion. Portions are given for three weight levels: small, medium and large dogs (see box below). For dogs in between these weights, you can adjust the amounts accordingly. For example, feed a 11-kg (25-lb) dog an amount midway between those for small and medium dogs, and a 27-kg (60-lb) dog an amount midway between those for medium and large dogs. Working dogs and other highly active dogs need more calories, so increase portion sizes or the amount of fat (especially for recipes that have low to moderate fat levels) in these recipes for these dogs. Watch your dog's weight and adjust the portions as needed to keep your dog slim.

DOG'S SIZE/WEIGHT	AMOUNT TO FEED (TWICE A DAY)
SMALL DOGS (6 kg/13 lb)	**250 CALORIES**
MEDIUM DOGS (16 kg/35 lb)	**500 CALORIES**
LARGE DOGS (36 kg/80 lb)	**1,000 CALORIES**

If you want your dog to lose weight, decrease the amount fed by no more than 10 per cent every two weeks until you begin to see weight loss, then continue to feed that amount. Slow and gradual weight loss is key; drastic changes in the amount of food fed will slow metabolism and make it harder for your dog to lose weight.

MAKING THE SWITCH

If your dog is prone to digestive upset, replace a small amount of commercial food with the new diet, then increase the amount every few days as long as your dog is doing well. If problems such as diarrhoea develop, revert to what you fed before and make the change even more slowly, using lower-fat foods.

PUPPIES, PREGNANCY & NURSING

Puppies and pregnant or nursing dogs have special nutritional needs – too much or too little calcium can result in serious health problems for example. The amount of calcium to add depends on the diet you feed, so it's difficult to give exact amounts that would apply to all diets, but adding 1,200–1,500 mg of calcium per 450 g (1 lb) of food to the recipes here should be safe for puppies.

VET'S ADVICE

Do not increase the amount of calcium given during pregnancy. Doing so can lead to eclampsia (calcium deficiency) after the puppies are born. It is fine to increase calcium amounts given while the puppies are nursing, but not before. In these special cases it may be safer to feed a dog food mix that is approved for puppies or for all life stages, combined with fresh foods according to their instructions. Always seek professional advice.

Supplements

Beneficial supplements include vitamins, minerals, herbs, probiotics and digestive enzymes. Most should be added at the time the food is served because some are affected by heating, freezing, light and air.

VITAMINS, MINERALS & FATTY ACIDS

The most important supplement to any diet is fish or salmon oil (not cod liver oil), which supplies omega-3 fatty acids that contribute to a healthy coat and skin and support for the immune system, the heart, kidneys and brain. A recommended starting dose of fish oil is 500 mg (small dogs) to 1,000 mg (large dogs), 1 to 2 times daily – and this dose applies to the amount of active omega-3s (EPA and DHA) noted on the label rather than to the amount of fish oil. Cod liver oil can be added to supply vitamins A and D; feed no more than 100 IUs (small dogs) to 400 IUs (large dogs) of vitamin D daily.

Whole food supplements may be optimal because the nutrients they supply work synergistically, but synthetics

LINSEED OIL

While linseed oil does provide benefits, neither linseed nor camelina oil is a good substitute for fish oil, since their omega-3 fatty acids are in a different form that is not readily utilized by dogs.

provide higher doses of vitamins and minerals. Green blends containing foods such as alfalfa, kelp, spirulina, parsley and chlorella are an excellent source of trace minerals and phytonutrients. Kelp is high in iodine, which is beneficial in small amounts but can suppress the thyroid if too much is given, so it's best to give kelp in very small amounts – ¼ teaspoon or less for a large dog.

Nutritional yeast (or brewer's yeast) supplies trace minerals, the B vitamins and other nutrients. You can add small amounts of raw honey, organic (unpasteurized) cider vinegar and ginger, which is especially good for digestion. Probiotics are useful after treatment with antibiotics and also for dogs prone to diarrhoea. Acidophilus is a good probiotic to add, but supplements that provide more than one kind of beneficial bacteria, especially Lactobacillus sporogenes and Enterococcus faecium, are even better. Some dogs with gastrointestinal problems may also benefit from digestive enzymes.

It's best to add a vitamin-mineral supplement to all home-made diets. There are a number of high-quality canine supplements available from holistic vets and high-end pet supply shops. Unfortunately, not all the supplements sold in most pet supply chain shops are as good. You can use supplements made for humans, adjusting the amounts to match the size of your dog. Rotating through different supplements offers advantages over always giving the same ones. Consult a veterinarian who supports home-made diets for more information.

Mary Straus, DogAware.com

Supplementing with Oils

Whenever you add oils to the diet, you also need to add a vitamin E supplement. Give your dog around 100 IUs per 9 kg (20 lb) of body weight daily, or every other day.

Snacks & Treats

From fruity ice lollies for a hot day to delicious training treats, here are a range of healthy snacks that your dog won't be able to resist.

Fruity Ice Lollies

Dogs just love the crunch of ice cubes, and here the rewards are made healthy and delicious. Perfect for a hot summer's day.

Facts

VET'S VIEW A fun and healthy treat, good for hot days and for teething puppies. It can also be frozen into stuffable chew toys (seal the tip with a blob of peanut butter first).

PORTION SIZE For small dogs, 1 cube; medium dogs, 2 cubes; large dogs, 4 cubes.

NUTRITIONAL INFORMATION
per cube

CALORIES	31
PROTEIN	0.2 g
CARBOHYDRATES	7.2 g
DIETARY FIBRE	0.1 g
FAT	0.2 g

Recipe

Preparation Time: 5 minutes   Makes: 24 ice cubes

- 🐾 **1.13 litres/2 pints fruit juice (not grape juice)**
- 🐾 **1 ripe banana, mashed**
- 🐾 **125 g/4 oz natural yogurt**

1 Blend the fruit juice with the mashed banana and mix in the yogurt.

2 Pour into ice-cube trays and put into the freezer.

3 When frozen, pop out of tray and serve one at a time.

Note The lollies will keep for up to 1 month in the freezer.

Liver Brownies

Brownies make great training treats, as they can be easily broken up into small pieces and they're soft enough to be eaten quickly.

Facts

VET'S VIEW Liver is packed with nutrients, especially vitamin A, as well as B vitamins, iron, zinc, selenium, copper and manganese.

PORTION SIZE For small dogs, ¼ brownie; medium dogs, ½ brownie; large dogs, 1 brownie. Break into pieces and feed each piece individually, as dogs are more excited by lots of small treats than by one large treat.

NUTRITIONAL INFORMATION
per brownie

CALORIES	169
PROTEIN	11 g
CARBOHYDRATES	22 g
DIETARY FIBRE	2.9 g
FAT	3.8 g

Recipe

Preparation Time: 10 minutes   Makes: about 12 brownies

- **450 g / 1 lb beef livers**
- **3 tbsp peanut butter**
- **250 g/9 oz wholemeal flour**
- **200 g/7 oz barley**

1 Cook the barley according to packet instructions.
2 Preheat oven to 180°C/350°F/Gas Mark 4.
3 Purée the livers in a food processor and mix in the peanut butter.
4 In a separate bowl, mix together the flour and the barley. Add to the liver mixture.
5 Pour the mixture into a 23 x 23 cm (9 x 9 inch) baking tin and bake for 20 minutes.

Note Leave to cool and cut into small pieces. Store in the fridge for 1 week.

Peanut Terrifics

Delicious and nutritious for your dog, these terrifics make fabulous training treats when broken into small pieces.

Facts

VET'S VIEW Peanut butter makes these treats highly attractive to dogs.

PORTION SIZE For small dogs, 1 treat; medium dogs, 2 treats; large dogs, 4 treats (can break into more while feeding).

NUTRITIONAL INFORMATION
per treat

CALORIES	31
PROTEIN	1.1 g
CARBOHYDRATES	4.2 g
DIETARY FIBRE	0.9 g
FAT	1.1 g

Recipe

Preparation Time: 10 minutes   Makes: about 24 treats

- 125 ml/4 fl oz water
- 3 tbsp peanut butter
- 150 g/5½ oz wholemeal flour

1 Preheat oven to 180°C/350°F/Gas Mark 4.
2 Mix all the ingredients together thoroughly.
3 Spread the mixture evenly on a baking tray and cut into desired shapes.
4 Bake for 30 minutes or until lightly browned and crisp.

Note: The terrifics will keep for 2–3 weeks in an airtight container.

Birthday Cupcakes

Treat the dog in your life to something tasty and healthful on his special day. A natural yogurt or cream cheese 'icing' makes a final touch.

Facts

VET'S VIEW These cupcakes are high in vitamin A and potassium, and will make a healthy treat your dog will love.

PORTION SIZE For small dogs, ¼ cupcake; medium dogs, ½ cupcake; large dogs, 1 cupcake (can break into pieces while feeding).

NUTRITIONAL INFORMATION
per cupcake

CALORIES	128
PROTEIN	2.7 g
CARBOHYDRATES	24 g
DIETARY FIBRE	2.7 g
FAT	2.7 g

Recipe

Preparation Time: 15 minutes Makes: about 12 cupcakes

- 175 g/6 oz wholemeal flour
- 1 tbsp baking powder
- 55 g/2 oz porridge oats
- 175 g/6 oz carrots, finely grated

- 125 ml/4 fl oz black treacle
- 125 ml/4 fl oz water
- 1 egg
- 1½ tbsp vegetable oil

1 Preheat oven to 180°C/350°F/Gas Mark 4.
2 Combine the flour, baking powder and oats in a small bowl.
3 Thoroughly combine the carrots, treacle, water, egg and oil in a large bowl.
4 Fold the dry ingredients into the wet and mix well.
5 Pour the mixture into the holes in a small 12-hole muffin tin and bake for 20 minutes.

Note: Store the Birthday Cupcakes in the fridge for 1 week.

Cinnamon Treasures

As an alternative to cinnamon, try flavouring these treats with powdered aniseed – few dogs can resist its aroma!

Facts

VET'S VIEW Chicken stock should make these treats appealing to your dog.

PORTION SIZE For small dogs, 1 treat; medium dogs, 2 treats; large dogs, 4 treats.

NUTRITIONAL INFORMATION
per treat

CALORIES	42
PROTEIN	1 g
CARBOHYDRATES	5.4 g
DIETARY FIBRE	1.1 g
FAT	1.9 g

Recipe

Preparation Time: 20 minutes Makes: about 36 treats

- 🐾 125 g/4½ oz wholemeal flour
- 🐾 125–140 g/4½–5 oz coarse oats
- 🐾 4 tbsp vegetable oil
- 🐾 225 ml/8 fl oz chicken stock
- 🐾 1 tbsp baking powder
- 🐾 200 g/7 oz raw carrots, finely grated
- 🐾 2 tbsp cinnamon

1 Preheat oven to 180°C/350°F/Gas Mark 4.
2 Mix together the flour and oats. Blend the vegetable oil, chicken stock, baking powder, carrots and cinnamon together.
3 Mix together the wet and dry ingredients, and spread the mixture evenly on to a baking tray. Cut into desired shapes.
4 Bake for 30 minutes or until lightly browned and crisp.

Note: Store in an airtight container for up to 2–3 weeks.

Meat & Potato Patties

Meat and potatoes aren't just a dinner staple – they can be used to make wholesome treats for your favourite pooch.

NUTRITIONAL INFORMATION
per patty

CALORIES	: 31
PROTEIN	: 1.8 g
CARBOHYDRATES	: 2.4 g
DIETARY FIBRE	: 0.2 g
FAT	: 1.6 g

Facts

VET'S VIEW These patties provide nutrition similar to a meal. For dogs counting calories, you can reduce meal size and feed part of the daily ration as treats.

PORTION SIZE For small dogs, 1 patty; for medium dogs, 2 patties; for large dogs, 4 patties.

Recipe

Preparation Time: 10 minutes   Makes: about 24 patties

- 🐾 **175 g/6 oz beef or chicken mince**
- 🐾 **85 g/3 oz carrots, grated**
- 🐾 **50 g/1¾ oz instant potato flakes**
- 🐾 **4 tbsp powdered milk**

1 Preheat oven to 180°C/ 350°F/Gas Mark 4.

2 Purée the meat and carrots in a food processor until smooth.

3 Thoroughly mix all the ingredients together.

4 Roll into small balls, press into patties and bake for 15 minutes or until firm.

Note: The patties will keep for 2 weeks in the fridge.

Autumn Bites

Pumpkin is a wonderful autumn treat to spoil your best friend with – and great for your dog's digestion too.

Facts

VET'S VIEW Tinned pumpkin purée can be used in place of fresh. Pumpkin is great for digestion, helping both to firm stools that are loose and to soften stools that are too hard.

PORTION SIZE For small dogs, 1 treat; for medium dogs, 2 treats; for large dogs, 4 treats.

NUTRITIONAL INFORMATION
per treat

CALORIES	35
PROTEIN	0.7 g
CARBOHYDRATES	6.1 g
DIETARY FIBRE	0.9 g
FAT	0.9 g

Recipe

Preparation Time: 15 minutes Makes: about 36 treats

- 🐾 **115 g/4 oz pumpkin purée (made from 1 lb/450 g fresh pumpkin, cooked and mashed)**
- 🐾 **4 tbsp black treacle**
- 🐾 **4 tbsp water**
- 🐾 **2 tbsp vegetable oil**
- 🐾 **250 g/9 oz wholemeal flour**
- 🐾 **1 tsp cinnamon**
- 🐾 **¼ tsp baking powder**
- 🐾 **¼ tsp bicarbonate of soda**

1 Preheat oven to 180°C/350°F/Gas Mark 4.
2 Blend together the pumpkin purée, treacle, water and vegetable oil.
3 Stir in the flour, cinnamon, baking powder and bicarbonate of soda to form a soft dough.
4 Roll the dough into balls, put on a baking tray, flatten them and prick with a fork.
5 Bake for 25 minutes, or until hard and crisp.

Note: Autumn Bites will keep up to 2 weeks in an airtight container.

Flea-be-gone Treats

Here's a tasty recipe you can use to treat your dog and help make him less attractive to fleas at the same time! Cut the treats into fancy shapes to make them more appealing.

Facts

VET'S VIEW Brewer's yeast may help to repel fleas. However, it's not a substitute for good flea control, especially for dogs allergic to flea bites.

PORTION SIZE For small dogs, 1 treat; for medium dogs, 2 treats; for large dogs, 4 treats.

NUTRITIONAL INFORMATION
per treat

CALORIES	35
PROTEIN	1.7 g
CARBOHYDRATES	5.2 g
DIETARY FIBRE	1.3 g
FAT	0.9 g

Recipe

Preparation Time: 15 minutes   Makes: about 24 treats

- 🐾 **125 g / 4½ oz wholemeal flour**
- 🐾 **55 g / 2 oz porridge oats**
- 🐾 **4 tbsp brewer's yeast**
- 🐾 **1 tbsp vegetable oil**
- 🐾 **125 ml / 4 fl oz beef stock**

1. Preheat oven to 190°C/375°F/Gas Mark 5.
2. Mix the dry ingredients together and set aside.
3. Mix the vegetable oil and beef stock together, then slowly add to the dry ingredients and mix well.
4. Roll dough to 5 mm (¼ inch) thick and cut into desired shapes.
5. Bake for 15–20 minutes or until firm and crisp.

Note: The treats will keep for 2 weeks in an airtight container.

Parsley & Salmon Kibbles

These delicious parsley and salmon treats are wheat- as well as meat-free, and will leave your dog asking for more.

Facts

VET'S VIEW Salmon is high in beneficial omega-3 fatty acids, while parsley is a good source of vitamin K.

PORTION SIZE For small dogs, ½ treat; for medium dogs, 1 treat; for large dogs, 2 treats.

NUTRITIONAL INFORMATION
per treat

CALORIES	108
PROTEIN	4 g
CARBOHYDRATES	17.9 g
DIETARY FIBRE	0.3 g
FAT	1.6 g

Recipe

Preparation Time: 10 minutes Makes: about 18 treats

- 175 g/6 oz tinned salmon, rinsed and drained
- 3 eggs
- 400 g/14 oz ground rice
- 30 g/1 oz fresh parsley, finely chopped (half the amount if using dried)

1 Preheat oven to 180°C/350°F/Gas Mark 4.
2 Blend all the ingredients in a food processor until a firm dough is formed.
3 Roll the dough to 5 mm (¼ inch) thick, cut into desired shapes and bake for 25 minutes until firm.

Note: The kibbles will keep for 2 weeks in the fridge.

Apple Treacle Delights

Your dog will love to chew on these delightful apple and treacle treats.

Facts

VET'S VIEW The rolled shape makes these treats fun for your dog to eat.

PORTION SIZE For small dogs, 1 treat; for medium dogs, 2 treats; for large dogs, 4 treats.

NUTRITIONAL INFORMATION per treat	
CALORIES	52
PROTEIN	1.3 g
CARBOHYDRATES	7.4 g
DIETARY FIBRE	1.3 g
FAT	2 g

Recipe

Preparation Time: 15 minutes   Makes: about 36 treats

- **250 g / 9 oz wholemeal flour**
- **55 g / 2 oz porridge oats**
- **1 apple, grated**
- **1 egg**
- **4 tbsp vegetable oil**
- **2 tbsp black treacle**
- **125 ml / 4 fl oz water**

1 Preheat oven to 180°C/350°F/Gas Mark 4.
2 Mix together the flour and oats.
3 Whisk together the apple, egg, vegetable oil, black treacle and water.
4 Slowly incorporate the dry ingredients into the wet and mix into a firm dough.
5 Roll the dough to 5 mm (¼ inch) thick, cut into desired shapes and bake for 30–35 minutes or until firm and crisp.

Note: The delights will keep up to 2 weeks in an airtight container.

Frozen Banana Treats

Frozen treats are great for keeping dogs cool in the summer, and they can be used to soothe teething pain in puppies.

Facts

VET'S VIEW Bananas are a great source of potassium. Combined with yogurt, they make a healthy treat. The mixture can also be frozen into stuffable chew toys (seal the tip with a blob of peanut butter first).

PORTION SIZE For small dogs, ½ treat; for medium dogs, 1 treat; for large dogs, 2 treats.

NUTRITIONAL INFORMATION per treat	
CALORIES	71
PROTEIN	3 g
CARBOHYDRATES	8.5 g
DIETARY FIBRE	0.7 g
FAT	3.1 g

Recipe

Preparation Time: 5 minutes   Makes: about 16 treats

🐾 **900 g/2 lb natural full-fat yogurt**

🐾 **2 tbsp peanut butter**

🐾 **3 ripe bananas, peeled and mashed**

1 Blend all the ingredients to a purée in a food processor.

2 Pour into 125-ml (4-fl oz) plastic cups.

3 Freeze until firm.

4 Pop the treat out of the cup and watch your dog enjoy!

Note: Store the treats in the freezer for up to 2 weeks.

Treacle Peanut Rewards

Treacle and peanut butter, two flavours that dogs love, combined in one healthy snack.

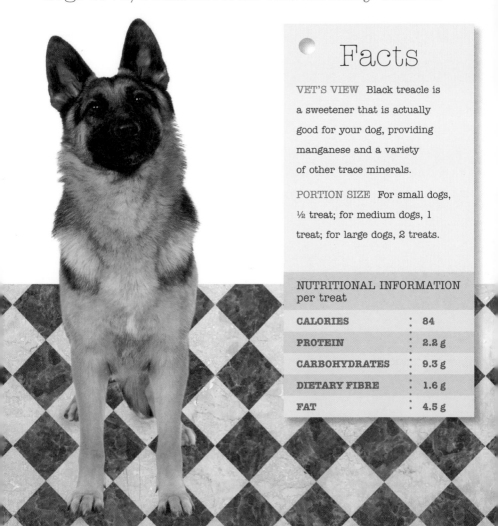

Facts

VET'S VIEW Black treacle is a sweetener that is actually good for your dog, providing manganese and a variety of other trace minerals.

PORTION SIZE For small dogs, ½ treat; for medium dogs, 1 treat; for large dogs, 2 treats.

NUTRITIONAL INFORMATION
per treat

CALORIES	84
PROTEIN	2.2 g
CARBOHYDRATES	9.3 g
DIETARY FIBRE	1.6 g
FAT	4.5 g

Recipe

Preparation Time: 15 minutes   Makes: about 36 treats

- **4 tbsp black treacle**
- **125 g/4 ½ oz peanut butter**
- **225 ml/8 fl oz water**
- **6 tbsp vegetable oil**
- **175 g/6 oz porridge oats**
- **250 g/9 oz wholemeal flour**

1 Preheat oven to 180°C/350°F/Gas Mark 4.
2 Whisk together the black treacle, peanut butter, water and vegetable oil.
3 Combine the oats and flour. Slowly add to the wet ingredients.
4 Mix thoroughly, drop tablespoonfuls onto a baking tray and press down.
5 Bake for 25–30 minutes or until firm.

Note: The rewards will keep up to 2 weeks in an airtight container.

Liver Biscuits

These biscuits contain paw-licking chicken liver. Cut them into fun shapes to please both you and your dog.

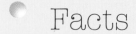

Facts

VET'S VIEW These biscuits are brimming with vitamin A, copper, selenium and other nutrients.

PORTION SIZE For small dogs, 1 treat; for medium dogs, 2 treats; for large dogs, 4 treats.

NUTRITIONAL INFORMATION
per treat

CALORIES	52
PROTEIN	3.1 g
CARBOHYDRATES	6.1 g
DIETARY FIBRE	1.2 g
FAT	1.6 g

Recipe

Preparation Time: 20 minutes Makes: about 36 treats

- 225 g/8 oz cooked chicken livers
- 2 tbsp vegetable oil
- 125 ml/4 fl oz chicken stock
- 2 tbsp chopped fresh parsley (or 2 tsp dried parsley)
- 250 g/9 oz wholemeal flour
- 85 g/3 oz porridge oats

1 Preheat oven to 180°C/350°F/Gas Mark 4.
2 Purée the chicken livers in a food processor.
3 Blend the vegetable oil, chicken stock and parsley with the liver purée, then mix in the flour and oats to form a firm dough.
4 Roll the dough to 5 mm (¼ inch) thick and cut into small bite-sized pieces.
5 Bake for 30 minutes or until firm and crisp.

Note: The Biscuits will keep for up to 2 weeks in the fridge.

Meaty Meals

Now for a hearty main
course – choose from turkey,
chicken, beef, duck, pork
and liver dishes. This section
contains dinner delights
for all breeds.

Hunter's Delight

Dogs are meat eaters just like us – try feeding venison as a special treat. It's lean, tasty and brimming with protein.

NUTRITIONAL INFORMATION
per portion

CALORIES	:	233
PROTEIN	:	32 g
CARBOHYDRATES	:	17 g
DIETARY FIBRE	:	2.1 g
FAT	:	3.3 g

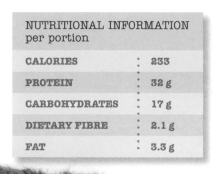

Facts

VET'S VIEW Venison is very lean, making this the lowest-fat recipe in this section, suitable for dogs that are inactive or have problems tolerating too much fat.

PORTION SIZE For small dogs, 1 portion; medium dogs, 2 portions; large dogs, 4 portions. Feed twice a day. See Amount to Feed on page 14 for more info.

CALCIUM Add 400 mg calcium per portion (600 mg if using bonemeal).

Recipe

Preparation Time: 15 minutes Makes: 9 portions

- 🐾 **900 g/2 lb venison**
- 🐾 **450 g/1 lb unpeeled potatoes, diced**
- 🐾 **225 g/8 oz tinned pears in juice, chopped**
- 🐾 **175 g/6 oz carrots, grated**

1 Preheat oven to 180°C/350°F/Gas Mark 4 and lightly oil a roasting tin.

2 Cut the venison into large chunks and mix with the potatoes. Put in the roasting tin and, if possible, insert a meat thermometer in one of the meat chunks.

3 Roast the venison and potatoes for about 25 minutes, or until the thermometer shows 74°C/165°F and the potatoes are tender.

4 Remove the venison and potatoes from the oven. Leave to cool.

5 Mix together the pears and carrots, and stir into the cooled meat and potatoes.

NOTES

For extra digestibility, stir in the carrot with the meat and potatoes 5 minutes before the end of cooking.

Farmer's Basket

Here is a simple recipe that can be used as a staple. Chicken, spinach, barley, egg and peanuts make a nutritious meal for your dog.

Facts

VET'S VIEW This low-fat, low-carb recipe is suitable for all dogs, including overweight dogs. Increase fat for more active dogs by including some of the skin from the chicken. Only serve dishes with spinach occasionally – it has a high oxalate content, which can cause urinary crystals in dogs.

PORTION SIZE For small dogs, ¾ portion; medium dogs, 1½ portions; large dogs, 3 portions. Feed twice a day. See Amount to Feed on page 14 for more info.

CALCIUM Add 400 mg calcium per portion (600 mg if using bonemeal).

NUTRITIONAL INFORMATION per portion	
CALORIES	340
PROTEIN	45 g
CARBOHYDRATES	6.1 g
DIETARY FIBRE	1.2 g
FAT	11 g

Recipe

Preparation Time: 20 minutes Makes: 10 portions

- 🐾 **1.3 kg/3 lb skinless chicken, whole or in pieces**
- 🐾 **175 g/6 oz barley**
- 🐾 **4 eggs**
- 🐾 **225 g/8 oz fresh spinach, torn**
- 🐾 **28 g/1 oz peanuts, chopped**

1 Preheat oven to 180°C/350°F/Gas Mark 4. Lightly oil a roasting tin.
2 Roast the chicken (breast or thigh, 20–30 minutes/whole chicken, 45–60 minutes) until the meat juices run clear when pierced with a skewer. Leave to cool.
3 Meanwhile, cook the barley according to packet instructions.
4 Remove the bones, and dice the meat into large pieces.
5 Lightly beat the eggs together, pour into a saucepan, add the spinach and cook for about 5 minutes until firm. Leave to cool.
6 Mix the egg with the chicken, barley and peanuts.

NOTES

Other types of nut can be substituted but never use macadamia nuts, which are toxic to dogs.

Autumn Fest

Facts

VET'S VIEW This recipe is suitable for all dogs, but you can reduce the carbs for overweight dogs. For active dogs, leave some of the skin on for more calories.

PORTION SIZE For small dogs, ¾ portion; medium dogs, 1½ portions; large dogs, 3 portions. Feed twice a day. See Amount to Feed on page 14 for more info.

CALCIUM Add 500 mg calcium per portion (750 mg if using bonemeal).

NUTRITIONAL INFORMATION
per portion

CALORIES	380
PROTEIN	36 g
CARBOHYDRATES	21 g
DIETARY FIBRE	2.2 g
FAT	16 g

Duck is a nice fatty meat that is beneficial to dogs – they like it too. Chicken liver and meat can also be used in place of duck.

Recipe

Preparation Time: 25 minutes Makes: 10 portions

- 🐾 **1.3 kg/3 lb skinless duck, whole or in pieces, light and dark meat**
- 🐾 **450 g/1 lb yams or sweet potatoes**
- 🐾 **225 g/8 oz duck livers**
- 🐾 **225 g/8 oz soup pasta**
- 🐾 **1–2 medium apples, cored and cubed**

1 Preheat the oven to 180°C/350°F/Gas Mark 4. Lightly oil a roasting tin.
2 Roast the duck (breast, 20–30 minutes/whole duck, 45–60 minutes) until the meat juices run clear when pierced with a skewer. Add fresh yams or sweet potatoes for the final 25–30 minutes of the cooking time. Leave to cool.
3 Put the duck livers in a pan with water to cover. Simmer over a medium-high heat for about 20 minutes. Leave to cool.
4 Cook the pasta according to packet instructions and drain well.
5 Remove all bones and cut the meat into large pieces.
6 Dice the livers and mix with the duck, pasta and apple.

Friday Night Supper

Here is a simple recipe with pork, beans, peas and rice that can use up some leftovers from the week's meals.

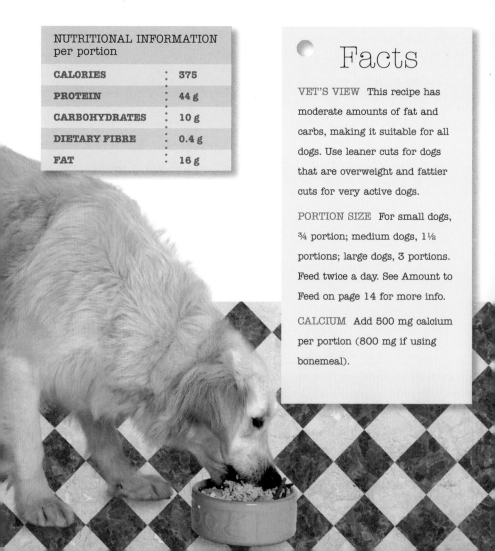

NUTRITIONAL INFORMATION per portion	
CALORIES	375
PROTEIN	44 g
CARBOHYDRATES	10 g
DIETARY FIBRE	0.4 g
FAT	16 g

Facts

VET'S VIEW This recipe has moderate amounts of fat and carbs, making it suitable for all dogs. Use leaner cuts for dogs that are overweight and fattier cuts for very active dogs.

PORTION SIZE For small dogs, ¾ portion; medium dogs, 1½ portions; large dogs, 3 portions. Feed twice a day. See Amount to Feed on page 14 for more info.

CALCIUM Add 500 mg calcium per portion (800 mg if using bonemeal).

Recipe

Preparation Time: 5 minutes Makes: 10 portions

- 🐾 **1.3 kg/3 lb pork meat**
- 🐾 **125 g/4 ½ oz cooked, chopped green beans or shelled peas**
- 🐾 **115 g/4 oz Cheddar cheese, grated**
- 🐾 **350 g/12 oz brown rice**

1 Cut the pork into large pieces and fry in a lightly sprayed pan over a medium heat for about 20 minutes until no longer pink and the meat juices run clear when pierced with a skewer.
2 Meanwhile, cook the rice according to packet instructions.
3 Remove the pan from the heat, add the cheese and leave to cool.
4 Stir the vegetables and rice into the meat mixture.

Italian Fest

We love Italian food and so does your dog. This is a hearty combination of beef, tomato, beans and pasta – plus Parmesan, of course.

Facts

VET'S VIEW This is the highest-fat recipe in this section, making it appropriate for working dogs and other very active dogs. Rinse fat from meat after cooking to make it suitable for less active and overweight dogs.

PORTION SIZE For small dogs, ½ portion; medium dogs, 1 portion; large dogs, 2 portions. Feed twice a day. See Amount to Feed on page 14 for more info.

CALCIUM Add 400 mg calcium per portion (600 mg if using bonemeal).

NUTRITIONAL INFORMATION per portion	
CALORIES	511
PROTEIN	43 g
CARBOHYDRATES	9.2 g
DIETARY FIBRE	0.7 g
FAT	33 g

Recipe

Preparation Time: 15 minutes   Makes: 8 portions

- 1.8 kg/4 lb lean beef mince or rump steak
- 1 medium tomato, diced
- 28 g/1 oz Parmesan cheese, grated
- 225 g/8 oz farfalle pasta
- 55 g/2 oz cooked, green beans, chopped

1. Fry the meat in a lightly sprayed pan over a medium heat for about 15 minutes until brown and the meat juices run clear.
2. Stir in the tomato and Parmesan. Remove from the heat. Leave to cool.
3. Meanwhile, cook the pasta according to the packet instructions. Drain well and add to the meat mixture.
4. Add the pasta and beans to the meat mixture. Leave to cool.

NOTES

Rotelle (spoke-wheel shaped) pasta is also great for this recipe.

Two-meat Dinner

The combo of chicken and beef gives your dog the best of both. Added liver makes this recipe tastier and highly nutritious as well.

Facts

VET'S VIEW This is a lower-fat, low-carb recipe suitable for all dogs. Increase fat for more active dogs by leaving some of the skin on the chicken.

PORTION SIZE For small dogs, ¾ portion; medium dogs, 1½ portions; large dogs, 3 portions. Feed twice a day. See Amount to Feed on page 14 for more info.

CALCIUM Add 500 mg calcium per portion (800 mg if using bonemeal).

NUTRITIONAL INFORMATION per portion		
CALORIES	:	325
PROTEIN	:	43 g
CARBOHYDRATES	:	8.7 g
DIETARY FIBRE	:	1.2 g
FAT	:	12 g

Recipe

Preparation Time: 20 minutes Makes: 12 portions

- 1.8 kg/4 lb skinless chicken, whole or in pieces, light and dark meat
- 225 g/8 oz beef livers
- 175 g/6 oz carrots, grated
- 350 g/12 oz barley
- 55 g/2 oz Cheddar cheese, grated

1 Preheat oven to 180°C/350°F/Gas Mark 4. Lightly oil a roasting tin.

2 Roast the chicken (breast or thigh, 20–30 minutes/whole chicken, 45–60 minutes) until the meat juices run clear when pierced with a skewer. Leave to cool.

3 Remove all bones and dice the meat into large pieces.

4 Put the beef livers in a saucepan with water to cover and simmer for 20 minutes, or until cooked through. Leave to cool.

5 Meanwhile, cook the barley according to packet instructions.

6 Dice the livers, mix with the chicken, carrots, barley and cheese.

NOTES
For extra digestibility, add the carrot to the pan 5 minutes before the end of cooking.

Christmas Dinner

This is a great meal to use up the leftovers from Christmas; dogs love the turkey and sweet potatoes too.

NUTRITIONAL INFORMATION
per portion

CALORIES	321
PROTEIN	44 g
CARBOHYDRATES	16 g
DIETARY FIBRE	1.9 g
FAT	7.7 g

Facts

VET'S VIEW This is a low-fat, moderate-carb recipe suitable for all dogs. Increase fat by including some skin from the turkey for more active dogs.

PORTION SIZE For small dogs, ¾ portion; medium dogs, 1½ portions; larger or more active dogs, 3 portions. Feed twice a day. See Amount to Feed on page 14 for more information.

CALCIUM Add 400 mg calcium per portion (600 mg if using bonemeal).

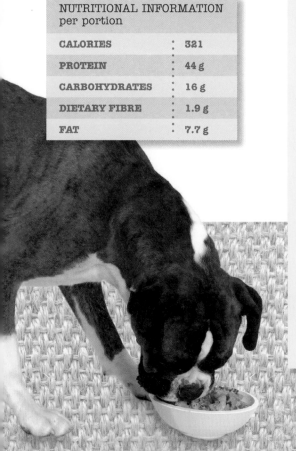

Recipe

Preparation Time: 30 minutes Makes: 9 portions

- 🐾 **1.3 kg / 3 lb skinless turkey pieces – light and dark meat**
- 🐾 **175 g / 6 oz coarse oats**
- 🐾 **450 g / 1 lb sweet potato cubes**
- 🐾 **2 tbsp cranberry sauce**
- 🐾 **4 tbsp turkey gravy**

1. Preheat oven to 180°C/350°F/Gas Mark 4. Oil a roasting tin.
2. Roast the turkey (boneless breast or thigh, 30–45 minutes/boned breast or thigh, 45–60 minutes/whole turkey, 1½–2 hours) until the juices run clear when pierced with a skewer. Add the potatoes for the final 30 minutes of the cooking time. Leave to cool.
3. Remove all the bones and dice the meat into large pieces. Peel and dice the sweet potatoes.
4. Meanwhile, cook the oats according to packet instructions.
5. Mix together the turkey meat, porridge, sweet potatoes and cranberry sauce. Pour the gravy over the mixture.

Bandit's Buffet

Here is a great recipe that includes offal – a great source of protein, so a good nutritional meat for dogs.

NUTRITIONAL INFORMATION per portion	
CALORIES	447
PROTEIN	47 g
CARBOHYDRATES	7.1 g
DIETARY FIBRE	0.9 g
FAT	24 g

Facts

VET'S VIEW This higher-fat, low-carb recipe can be used for active dogs. Use leaner meats for inactive and overweight dogs.

PORTION SIZE For small dogs, ⅝ portion; medium dogs, 1¼ portions; large dogs, 2½ portions. Feed twice a day. See Amount to Feed on page 14 for more info.

CALCIUM Add 500 mg calcium per person (750 mg if using bonemeal).

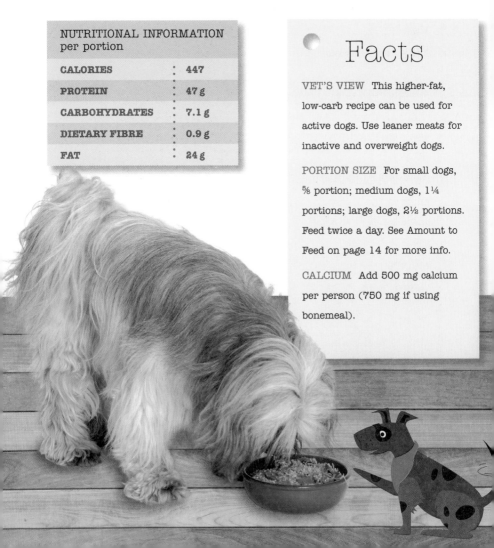

Recipe

Preparation Time: 15 minutes Makes: 10 portions

- 1.3 kg/3 lb pork mince
- 1.3 kg/3 lb heart
- 175 g/6 oz quinoa
- 85 g/3 oz carrots, grated
- 1 medium apple, cubed

1 Fry the pork in a lightly sprayed pan over a medium heat for about 15 minutes until no longer pink and the meat juices run clear when pierced with a skewer.

2 Meanwhile, cook the quinoa according to packet instructions.

3 Put the heart in a large saucepan with water to cover, and simmer for 45–60 minutes until cooked through. It should still be firm to the touch.

4 Drain the heart and leave to cool, then cut into small pieces.

5 Mix the pork and heart with the quinoa, and set aside.

6 Mix together the carrots and apple. Fold into the pork mixture.

NOTES

For extra digestibility, stir in the carrot with the heart 5 minutes before the end of cooking.

Chicken Delight

A refreshing meal with meat and fruit topped with healthful yogurt.

Facts

VET'S VIEW This recipe has low to moderate fat and low carbs, making it suitable for all dogs. For active dogs, increase fat by leaving some of the skin on the chicken.

PORTION SIZE For small dogs, ⅞ portion; medium dogs, 1¾ portions; large dogs, 3½ portions. Feed twice a day. See Amount to Feed on page 14 for more info.

CALCIUM Add 400 mg calcium per person (600 mg if using bonemeal).

NUTRITIONAL INFORMATION
per portion

CALORIES	300
PROTEIN	41 g
CARBOHYDRATES	7.3 g
DIETARY FIBRE	0.7 g
FAT	11 g

Recipe

Preparation Time: 20 minutes Makes: 10 portions

- 🐾 **1.3 kg/3 lb chicken, whole or pieces, light and dark meat**
- 🐾 **225 g/8 oz chicken livers**
- 🐾 **225 g/8 oz tinned peaches in natural juice**
- 🐾 **225 g/8 oz tinned pears in natural juice**
- 🐾 **225 g/8 oz natural full-fat yogurt**

1. Preheat oven to 180°C/350°F/Gas Mark 4. Lightly oil a roasting tin. Roast the chicken (breast or thigh, 20–30 minutes/whole chicken, 45–60 minutes) until the meat juices run clear when pierced with a skewer. Leave to cool.
2. Remove all the bones and dice the chicken into large pieces.
3. Put the livers in a saucepan with water to cover, and simmer over a medium-high heat for about 20 minutes or until cooked through. Leave to cool.
4. Cut the livers into pieces and mix with the chicken. Add the fruit pieces and yogurt.

Western Stew

A hearty meal for man's best friend, the rich flavours of buffalo and spinach are blended together in this meal fit for a king.

Facts

VET'S VIEW Buffalo is very lean, suitable for dogs with fat intolerance, while beef is much higher in fat. Nutritional information is based on using lean beef, so increase portions if using buffalo instead. Only serve dishes with spinach occasionally – it has a high oxalate content, which can cause urinary crystals in dogs.

PORTION SIZE For small dogs, ¾ portion; medium dogs, 1½ portions; large dogs, 3 portions. Feed twice a day. See Amount to Feed on page 14 for more info.

CALCIUM Add 400 mg calcium per portion (600 mg if using bonemeal).

NUTRITIONAL INFORMATION per portion	
CALORIES	381
PROTEIN	30 g
CARBOHYDRATES	12 g
DIETARY FIBRE	1.7 g
FAT	23 g

Recipe

Preparation Time: 15 minutes Makes: 8 portions

- 🐾 1.3 kg/3 lb buffalo or lean beef, cubed
- 🐾 175 g/6 oz coarse oats
- 🐾 175 g/6 oz barley
- 🐾 225 g/8 oz tinned peaches in natural juice
- 🐾 115 g/4 oz fresh spinach leaves, torn

1 Fry the meat in a lightly sprayed pan over a medium heat for about 15 minutes until browned and the meat juices run clear when pierced with a skewer. Leave to cool.

2 Cook the oats and barley according to packet instructions. Mix them together and add the meat.

3 Chop the peaches and stir into the mixture with the spinach.

NOTES
Lightly cooking the spinach leaves with the meat adds to its nutritional value and also makes them more digestible.

Coral's Caribbean Treat

This sweet little meal is wonderful for those hot summer days or as a treat in the winter months.

Facts

VET'S VIEW This recipe is relatively low in fat and carbs, making it suitable for all dogs. Note that light chicken meat is very low in fat, while dark meat is fattier.

PORTION SIZE For small dogs, ⅞ portion; medium dogs, 1¾ portions; large dogs, 3½ portions. Feed twice a day. See Amount to Feed on page 14 for more info.

CALCIUM Add 400 mg calcium per portion (600 mg if using bonemeal).

NUTRITIONAL INFORMATION per portion

CALORIES	312
PROTEIN	40 g
CARBOHYDRATES	11 g
DIETARY FIBRE	0.5 g
FAT	11 g

Recipe

Preparation Time: 30 minutes   Makes: 9 portions

- 🐾 1.3 kg/3 lb skinless chicken, whole or pieces, light and dark meat
- 🐾 1 medium sweet potato
- 🐾 225 g/8 oz soup pasta
- 🐾 225 g/8 oz cantaloupe melon, diced
- 🐾 125 g/4 oz natural full-fat yogurt

1 Preheat oven to 180°C/350°F/Gas Mark 4.

2 Lightly oil a roasting tin. Roast the chicken (breast or thigh, 20–30 minutes/whole chicken, 45–60 minutes) until the meat juices run clear when pierced with a skewer. Add the sweet potato for the final 25–30 minutes of the cooking time. Leave to cool.

3 Meanwhile, cook the pasta according to packet instructions.

4 Remove all the bones and dice the meat into large pieces. Peel and cube the sweet potato.

5 Mix with the pasta, and top with the melon and yogurt.

Sweet & Simple Liveicious

Facts

VET'S VIEW This recipe is higher in fat, which is good for active dogs. Rinse fat from meat after cooking to make it suitable for less active and overweight dogs.

PORTION SIZE For small dogs, ⅝ portion; medium dogs, 1¼ portions; large dogs, 2½ portions. Feed twice a day. See Amount to Feed on page 14 for more info.

CALCIUM Add 400 mg calcium per portion (600 mg if using bonemeal).

This simple and easy liver dinner is enhanced with the flavours of apples and pumpkin.

NUTRITIONAL INFORMATION
per portion

CALORIES	416
PROTEIN	37 g
CARBOHYDRATES	6.9 g
DIETARY FIBRE	1.8 g
FAT	26 g

Recipe

Preparation Time: 20 minutes Makes: 8 portions

- 🐾 **1.3 kg/3 lb lean beef mince**
- 🐾 **225 g/8 oz beef livers**
- 🐾 **225 g/8 oz tinned pumpkin**
- 🐾 **1 medium apple, diced**
- 🐾 **125 g/4½ oz cooked, green beans, chopped, or shelled peas**

1. Fry the beef mince in a lightly sprayed pan over a medium heat for about 15 minutes until brown and the juices run clear. Leave to cool.
2. Put the livers in a saucepan with water to cover and simmer over a medium-high heat for about 20 minutes or until cooked through. Leave to cool.
3. Dice the livers and mix with the beef mince.
4. Mash the pumpkin, mix with the apple and green beans, and add to the meat mixture.

Lighter Meals

Fish, eggs and cottage cheese can be used to create healthy meatless meals. Never feed dogs a vegan diet, as they require nutrients only found in animal products.

Spring Dinner

A tasty meal that contains tuna and fresh asparagus – the perfect springtime treat for your canine companion.

Facts

VET'S VIEW Fresh tuna and tuna packed in oil supply a moderate amount of fat. Tuna in olive oil is the best choice if using tinned tuna.

PORTION SIZE For small dogs, ¾ portion; medium dogs, 1½ portions; large dogs, 3 portions. Feed twice a day. See Amount to Feed on page 14 for more info.

CALCIUM Add 500 mg calcium per portion (900 mg if using bonemeal).

NUTRITIONAL INFORMATION
per portion

CALORIES	326
PROTEIN	40 g
CARBOHYDRATES	14 g
DIETARY FIBRE	0.6 g
FAT	11 g

Recipe

Preparation Time: 15 minutes Makes: 7 portions

- 900 g / 2 lb tuna (fresh or tinned in oil)
- 350 g / 12 oz brown rice
- 140–175 g / 5–6 oz cooked asparagus, chopped
- 2 tbsp chopped fresh parsley

1 If using fresh tuna, bake at 180°C/350°F/Gas Mark 4 for about 10–15 minutes until it flakes easily. Leave to cool and remove any bones.
2 If using tinned tuna, do not drain.
3 Cook the rice according to packet instructions.
4 Mix together the tuna, brown rice and asparagus.
5 Sprinkle the parsley over the top.

NOTES
Use either fresh or tinned tuna. If fresh, be sure no bones are present.

Tuna & Potato Dinner

Tuna and potato is a great easy meal, served here with carrots and yogurt. The fish oil will give your dog a beautifully shiny coat.

Facts

VET'S VIEW Portion size is based on using fresh tuna or tuna packed in oil. Tuna packed in water is lower in fat and calories, suitable only for dogs with fat intolerance and requiring increased portion size.

PORTION SIZE For small dogs, ¾ portion; medium dogs, 1½ portions; large dogs, 3 portions. Feed twice a day. See Amount to Feed on page 14 for more info.

CALCIUM Add 500 mg calcium per portion (800 mg if using bonemeal).

NUTRITIONAL INFORMATION per portion		
CALORIES	:	334
PROTEIN	:	37 g
CARBOHYDRATES	:	13 g
DIETARY FIBRE	:	1.5 g
FAT	:	14 g

Recipe

Preparation Time: 15 minutes   Makes: 7½ portions

- 900 g/2 lb tuna (fresh or packed in oil)
- 350 g/12 oz baking potato, diced
- 2 tbsp olive oil
- 175 g/6 oz carrots, grated
- 4 tbsp natural full-fat yogurt

1. If using fresh tuna, bake at 180°C/350°F/Gas Mark 4 for 10–15 minutes until it flakes easily. Carefully remove any bones. Leave to cool.
2. If using tinned tuna, do not drain.
3. Bake the potato at 180°C/350°F/Gas Mark 4 for about 30 minutes until tender; leave to cool, dice, leaving the skin on.
4. Mix together the tuna, potato, olive oil, carrots and yogurt.

NOTES

Be sure to remove any green spots from potatoes, as they are poisonous.

Raw carrot is fine, but lightly cooking it makes it more digestible.

Morgan's Salmon Special

Salmon is an excellent way to include the omega-3 fatty acids that help create a wonderful, healthy, shiny coat.

Facts

VET'S VIEW You may substitute tinned salmon. The bones in tinned fish are pressure-cooked to softness, so they can be fed. Farmed salmon is higher in fat than wild salmon.

PORTION SIZE For small dogs, 1 portion; medium dogs, 2 portions; large dogs, 4 portions. Feed twice a day. See Amount to Feed on page 14 for more info.

CALCIUM Add 400 mg calcium per portion (600 mg if using bonemeal). Add half when feeding tinned fish with bones.

NUTRITIONAL INFORMATION per portion	
CALORIES	270
PROTEIN	29 g
CARBOHYDRATES	13 g
DIETARY FIBRE	1.5 g
FAT	10 g

Recipe

Preparation Time: 10 minutes Makes: 5¾ portions

- 🐾 **900 g/2 lb salmon fillets**
- 🐾 **175 g/6 oz brown rice**
- 🐾 **125 g/4½ oz cooked, shelled peas**
- 🐾 **125 g/4 oz natural full-fat yogurt**

1 Poach the salmon for 15–20 minutes until it flakes easily. Leave to cool and carefully remove any bones.
2 Meanwhile, cook the rice according to packet instructions.
3 Mix together the salmon, brown rice and peas.
4 Spread the yogurt on top of the salmon mixture.

Salmon & Sweet Potatoes

Facts

VET'S VIEW This recipe has moderate fat and carbs, making it suitable for all dogs. Farmed salmon is higher in fat than wild salmon. Tinned salmon is usually wild.

PORTION SIZE For small dogs, 1 portion; medium dogs, 2 portions; large dogs, 4 portions. Feed twice a day. See Amount to Feed on page 14 for more info.

CALCIUM Add 400 mg calcium per portion (600 mg if using bonemeal). Add half when feeding tinned fish with bones.

NUTRITIONAL INFORMATION
per portion

CALORIES	250
PROTEIN	26 g
CARBOHYDRATES	14 g
DIETARY FIBRE	1.0 g
FAT	9.5 g

Dogs go crazy over sweet potatoes and love the salmon garnished with yogurt.

Recipe

Preparation Time: 20 minutes Makes: 6¼ portions

- 🐾 **900 g / 2 lb salmon fillet**
- 🐾 **1 medium sweet potato**
- 🐾 **125 g / 4½ oz cooked green beans, chopped**
- 🐾 **175 g / 6 oz brown rice**
- 🐾 **125 g / 4 oz natural full-fat yogurt**

1 Poach the salmon fillet for 15–20 minutes until it flakes easily. Leave to cool and carefully remove any bones.

2 Bake the sweet potato at 180°C/350°F/Gas Mark 4 for about 30 minutes until tender. Leave to cool. Peel and discard the skin, and dice the flesh.

3 Meanwhile, cook the rice according to packet instructions.

4 Mix together the salmon, sweet potato, green beans and brown rice.

5 Spread the yogurt on top of the salmon mixture.

Autumn Omelette

This is a nice quick meal that you can put together at the same time as your breakfast. Dogs love the taste of pumpkin, and it is good for their coat too.

NUTRITIONAL INFORMATION per portion	
CALORIES	240
PROTEIN	18 g
CARBOHYDRATES	17 g
DIETARY FIBRE	1.9 g
FAT	11 g

Facts

VET'S VIEW Pumpkin supplies fibre that can either firm up or loosen stools. Reduce the amount of pumpkin if your dog has loose stools with this recipe.

PORTION SIZE For small dogs, 1 portion; medium dogs, 2 portions; large dogs, 4 portions. Feed twice a day. See Amount to Feed on page 14 for more info.

CALCIUM Add 300 mg calcium per portion (500 mg if using bonemeal).

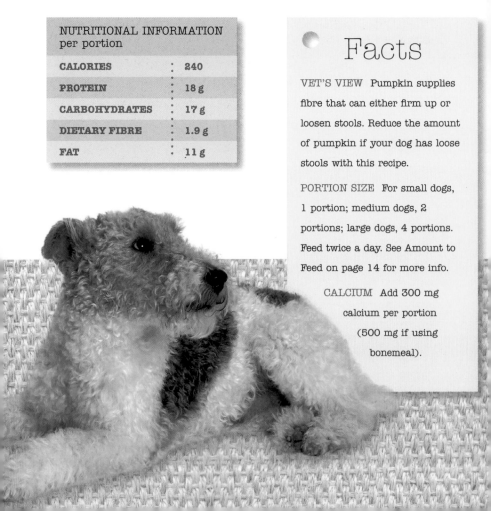

Recipe

Preparation Time: 20 minutes Makes: 6¾ portions

- 675 g / 1 lb 8oz full-fat cottage cheese
- 2 ripe bananas, mashed
- 225 g / 8 oz pumpkin purée
- 3–4 slices tinned peaches in natural juice
- 6 eggs

1 Mix together the cottage cheese, mashed bananas and pumpkin purée.
2 Fold the peach slices into the cottage cheese mixture. Set aside.
3 Lightly beat the eggs together and cook in a frying pan for about 5 minutes until no longer runny. Leave to cool.
4 Place the cooked egg in the feeding bowl and top with the cottage cheese mixture.

NOTES
If using tinned pumpkin, use plain pumpkin that has not been sweetened.

Nemo's Fish Special

Mackerel is a great fish to feed because of its fatty acids – and yogurt aids good digestion.

NUTRITIONAL INFORMATION per portion	
CALORIES	248
PROTEIN	29 g
CARBOHYDRATES	11 g
DIETARY FIBRE	1.8 g
FAT	9.1 g

Facts

VET'S VIEW You may substitute tinned mackerel, which is usually sourced responsibly – look for the Marine Stewardship Council logo. Mercury levels are not a concern with small fish such as these, or with salmon, trout and whitefish.

PORTION SIZE For small dogs, 1 portion; medium dogs, 2 portions; large dogs, 4 portions. Feed twice a day. See Amount to Feed on page 14 for more info.

CALCIUM Add 400 mg calcium per portion (600 mg if using bonemeal). Add only half this amount of calcium when feeding tinned fish with bones.

Recipe

Preparation Time: 15 minutes Makes: 6¾ portions

- 900g/2 lb mackerel fillets
- 1 medium sweet potato
- 125 g/4½ oz cooked, shelled peas
- 450 g/1 lb natural full-fat yogurt
- 2 tbsp chopped fresh dill

1 Bake the mackerel at 180°C/350°F/Gas Mark 4 for 15 minutes until it flakes easily. Leave to cool and then remove any bones.

2 Bake the sweet potato at 180°C/350°F/Gas Mark 4 for about 30 minutes until tender. Leave to cool, remove the skin and dice.

3 Mix together the mackerel, sweet potato and peas and put in the feeding bowl.

4 Mix the yogurt with the dill and spread on top of the mackerel mixture.

Friday Night Fish & Chips

Beetroot adds a nice touch to this spin on fish and chips.

Facts

VET'S VIEW This moderate-fat diet is suitable for all dogs. Fish won't keep long in the fridge, so extras should be frozen for future meals.

PORTION SIZE For small dogs, ¾ portion; medium dogs, 1½ portions; large dogs, 3 portions. Feed twice a day. See Amount to Feed on page 14 for more info.

CALCIUM Add 600 mg calcium per portion (1,100 mg if using bonemeal).

NUTRITIONAL INFORMATION
per portion

CALORIES	325
PROTEIN	37 g
CARBOHYDRATES	10 g
DIETARY FIBRE	1.1 g
FAT	14 g

Recipe

Preparation Time: 25 minutes   Makes: 7 portions

- 🐾 **900g/2 lb pollack, or other white fish**
- 🐾 **1 medium potato**
- 🐾 **1 large or 2 small beetroot**
- 🐾 **85 oz/3 oz carrots, grated**
- 🐾 **4 eggs**
- 🐾 **4 tbsp natural full-fat yogurt**

1 Bake the pollack at 180°C/350°F/Gas Mark 4 for 15–20 minutes until it flakes easily. Leave to cool and remove all bones.

2 Roast the potato and beetroot together at 180°C/350°F/Gas Mark 4 for 30–35 minutes until tender. Leaving the skin on, dice the potato, then peel and dice the beetroot.

3 Mix together the fish, potato, beetroot and carrots.

4 Lightly beat the eggs, and cook in a fying pan for about 5 minutes until no longer runny. Leave to cool.

5 Fold the eggs into the fish mixture and top with the yogurt.

NOTES
Raw carrot is fine, but lightly cooking it makes it more digestible.

Lakeside Dinner

Facts

VET'S VIEW Tinned salmon or mackerel may be substituted for trout. This recipe has more carbs than most, which you may want to limit for overweight dogs.

PORTION SIZE For small dogs, 1 portion; medium dogs, 2 portions; large dogs, 4 portions. Feed twice a day. See Amount to Feed on page 14 for more info.

CALCIUM Add 400 mg calcium per portion (700 mg if using bonemeal). Add only half this amount of calcium when feeding tinned fish with bones.

NUTRITIONAL INFORMATION
per portion

CALORIES	271
PROTEIN	29 g
CARBOHYDRATES	16 g
DIETARY FIBRE	1.0 g
FAT	9.3 g

Trout and pasta give this dish great flavour, accompanied by a peach, carrot and yogurt mix, which is good for digestion.

Recipe

Preparation Time: 10 minutes   Makes: 9½ portions

- 900 g / 2 lb trout fillets
- 450 g / 1 lb stelline (tiny star-shaped pasta) or soup pasta
- 3–4 slices tinned peaches, in natural juice, diced
- 175 g / 6 oz carrots, grated
- 225 g / 8 oz natural full-fat yogurt

1 Poach the trout for about 20 minutes until it flakes easily. Leave to cool, then carefully remove any bones.
2 Meanwhile, cook the pasta according to packet instructions.
3 Mix together with the pasta, peaches, carrots and yogurt.
4 Flake the trout into the pasta mixture.

Chef's Salad

Just as salads are good for people, this spinach-based vegetable mixture is a great meal for your healthy hound.

NUTRITIONAL INFORMATION per portion	
CALORIES	285
PROTEIN	33 g
CARBOHYDRATES	15 g
DIETARY FIBRE	0.8 g
FAT	9.6 g

Facts

VET'S VIEW You shouldn't feed spinach too frequently due to its high oxalate content, so rotate between spinach and other green leafy vegetables when preparing this recipe.

PORTION SIZE For small dogs, ⅞ portion; medium dogs, 1¾ portions; large dogs, 3½ portions. Feed twice a day. See Amount to Feed on page 14 for more info.

CALCIUM Add 400 mg calcium per portion (800 mg if using bonemeal).

Recipe

Preparation Time: 15 minutes Makes: 8½ portions

- 🐾 **900 g/2 lb tuna (fresh or tinned in oil)**
- 🐾 **350 g/12 oz brown rice**
- 🐾 **1 large pear, peeled, cored and sliced**
- 🐾 **115 g/4 oz fresh spinach, torn**
- 🐾 **85 g/3 oz carrots, grated**
- 🐾 **4 tbsp natural full-fat yogurt**

1 For fresh tuna, bake at 180°C/350°F/Gas Mark 4 for 10–15 minutes until it flakes easily. Leave to cool. Remove any bones.

2 If using tinned tuna, do not drain.

3 Cook the rice according to packet instructions.

4 Mix together the tuna and brown rice. Set aside.

5 Mix together the pear, spinach and carrots.

6 Fold the tuna mixture and fresh ingredients mixture together.

7 Put in the feeding bowl and top with the yogurt.

NOTES
Serving raw veg is fine, but lightly cooking them makes them more digestible.

Mackerel & Egg Breakfast

A twist on steak and eggs, this mackerel and eggs meal is great for breakfast or dinner.

Facts

VET'S VIEW Two tins of mackerel can be substituted for 900 g (2 lb) fresh. The salt in tinned fish is not harmful, but you can rinse the fish if a low-sodium diet is required.

PORTION SIZE For small dogs, ¾ portion; medium dogs, 1½ portions; large dogs, 3 portions. Feed twice a day. See Amount to Feed on page 14 for more info.

CALCIUM Add 400 mg calcium per portion (600 mg if using bonemeal). Add only half this amount of calcium when feeding tinned fish with bones.

NUTRITIONAL INFORMATION per portion	
CALORIES	309
PROTEIN	37 g
CARBOHYDRATES	5.6 g
DIETARY FIBRE	0.8 g
FAT	14 g

Recipe

Preparation Time: 25 minutes   Makes: 6 portions

- 🐾 **900 g / 2 lb mackerel fillets**
- 🐾 **225 g / 8 oz cottage cheese**
- 🐾 **4 eggs**
- 🐾 **55 g / 2 oz cooked, shelled peas**
- 🐾 **3–4 slices tinned peaches in natural juice**

1 Bake the mackerel at 180°C/350°F/Gas Mark 4 for about 15 minutes until it flakes easily. Leave to cool and carefully remove any bones.

2 Mix together the cottage cheese, peas and peaches.

3 Lightly beat the eggs and cook in a frying pan for about 5 minutes until no longer runny.

4 Fold the scrambled eggs into the cottage cheese mixture and put in the feeding bowl.

5 Flake the mackerel on top.

On the Go
Eggs & Potatoes

This egg-based dish also includes fruit for a sweet blend; the eggs make a good, nutritious meal.

Facts

VET'S VIEW This recipe won't freeze well, so it's best to mix together only what will be consumed at one time. Eggs can also be soft-cooked, poached or hard-boiled.

PORTION SIZE For small dogs, 1 portion; medium dogs, 2 portions; large dogs, 4 portions. Feed twice a day. See Amount to Feed on page 14 for more info.

CALCIUM Add 400 mg calcium per portion (500 mg if using bonemeal).

NUTRITIONAL INFORMATION
per portion

CALORIES	240
PROTEIN	17 g
CARBOHYDRATES	17 g
DIETARY FIBRE	1.4 g
FAT	11 g

Recipe

Preparation Time: 15 minutes Makes: 8 portions

- 8 eggs
- 225 g/8 oz cantaloupe melon, diced
- 675 g/1½ lb cottage cheese
- 1 medium baking potato
- 225 g/8 oz tinned pears in natural juice, sliced

1 Lightly beat the eggs and cook in a frying pan for about 5 minutes until no longer runny. Leave to cool.
2 Bake the potato at 180°C/350°F/Gas Mark 4 for about 30 minutes until tender. Leave to cool and dice, leaving skin on.
3 Mix together the scrambled eggs and potatoes.
4 Stir in the cottage cheese, melon and pears.

Salmon Pasta in Yogurt Dill Sauce

Salmon is a wonderfully nutritious meal for dogs, and this one has a delicious dill and yogurt garnish.

NUTRITIONAL INFORMATION per portion	
CALORIES	223
PROTEIN	21 g
CARBOHYDRATES	17 g
DIETARY FIBRE	1.2 g
FAT	7.2 g

Facts

VET'S VIEW Two large tins of tinned salmon can be substituted for 900 g (2 lb) fresh. Pasta amount may be reduced for dogs that are overweight.

PORTION SIZE For small dogs, 1⅛ portions; medium dogs, 2¼ portions; large dogs, 4½ portions. Feed twice a day. See Amount to Feed on page 14 for more info.

CALCIUM Add 400 mg calcium per portion (600 mg if using bonemeal). Add only half this amount of calcium when feeding tinned fish with bones.

Recipe

Preparation Time: 15 minutes Makes: 8½ portions

- 900 g / 2 lb salmon fillets
- 450 g / 1 lb soup pasta or similar small pasta shapes
- 55 g / 2 oz cooked green beans, chopped
- 175 g / 6 oz carrots, grated
- 125 g / 4 oz natural full-fat yogurt
- 2 tbsp chopped fresh dill

1 Poach the salmon for 15–20 minutes until it flakes easily. Leave to cool. Carefully remove any bones.

2 Meanwhile, cook the pasta according to packet instructions.

3 Mix together the beans, carrots, yogurt and dill.

4 Flake the salmon and mix with the pasta.

5 Fold the vegetable mixture into the salmon-pasta mixture.

Doggy Delicious Omelette

Facts

VET'S VIEW This high-fat diet is suitable for very active dogs. Reduce the amount of cheese for less active and overweight dogs. Prepare only an amount that will be consumed at one time.

PORTION SIZE For small dogs, ¾ portion; medium dogs, 1½ portions; large dogs, 3 portions. Feed twice a day. See Amount to Feed on page 14 for more info.

CALCIUM Add 500 mg calcium per portion (800 mg if using bonemeal).

NUTRITIONAL INFORMATION
per portion

CALORIES	360
PROTEIN	22 g
CARBOHYDRATES	9.8 g
DIETARY FIBRE	0.9 g
FAT	26 g

Your pup will love this omelette. The mixture of sweet potatoes and spinach packs lots of nutritional punch.

Recipe

Preparation Time: 20 minutes Makes: 5½ portions

- 🐾 **8 eggs**
- 🐾 **225 g / 8 oz Cheddar cheese**
- 🐾 **1 medium sweet potato**
- 🐾 **115 g / 4 oz fresh spinach, torn**
- 🐾 **225 g / 8 oz natural full-fat yogurt**

1 Lightly beat the eggs and cook in a frying pan for about 5 minutes until no longer runny. Leave to cool.

2 Coarsely grate the cheese and mix with the scrambled eggs.

3 Bake the sweet potato at 180°C/350°F/Gas Mark 4 for about 30 minutes until tender. Leave to cool, then peel and dice the flesh.

4 Mix the sweet potato into the egg and cheese.

5 Mix together with the spinach and the yogurt and serve immediately.

NOTES

Raw spinach is fine, but lightly cooking it makes it more digestible. Only serve spinach occasionally, as the leaves have a high oxalate content.

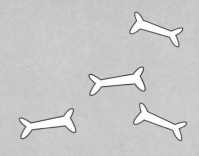

Special Diets

Certain ingredients can help dogs with problems such as fleas or bad breath. Diet alone is not always a cure, though, so always discuss health issues with your vet.

Beefy Dinner

The brewer's yeast in this recipe may assist in keeping those pesky fleas at bay. Make sure that you use lean beef mince.

Facts

VET'S VIEW Brewer's yeast provides B vitamins that may deter fleas, but is not a substitute for a good flea control programme.

PORTION SIZE For small dogs, ½ portion; medium dogs, 1 portion; large dogs, 2 portions. Feed twice a day. See Amount to Feed on page 14.

CALCIUM Add 400 mg calcium per portion (600 mg if using bonemeal).

NUTRITIONAL INFORMATION
per portion

CALORIES	529
PROTEIN	39 g
CARBOHYDRATES	11 g
DIETARY FIBRE	2.5 g
FAT	36 g

Recipe

Preparation Time: 10 minutes   Makes: 6 portions

- 🐾 1.3 kg/3 lb lean beef mince
- 🐾 2 tbsp brewer's yeast
- 🐾 175 g/6 oz brown rice

- 🐾 55 g/2 oz cooked green beans, chopped
- 🐾 85 g/3 oz carrots, grated

1 Fry the beef mince in a lightly sprayed pan over a medium heat for about 20 minutes until no longer pink and the meat juices run clear. Set aside and leave to cool.

2 Meanwhile, cook the rice according to packet instructions.

3 Mix together the brewer's yeast, rice, green beans and carrots.

4 Add the beef when cool.

5 Store leftovers in the fridge.

Turkey Dinner

Adding cider vinegar to a great turkey dinner may help with reducing fleas.

Facts

VET'S VIEW Unpasteurized organic cider vinegar provides more nutritional benefit.

PORTION SIZE For small dogs, ¾ portion; medium dogs, 1½ portions; large dogs, 3 portions. Feed twice a day. See Amount to Feed, page 14 for more info.

CALCIUM Add 400 mg calcium per portion (600 mg if using bonemeal).

NUTRITIONAL INFORMATION per portion	
CALORIES	368
PROTEIN	29 g
CARBOHYDRATES	6.8 g
DIETARY FIBRE	1.1 g
FAT	24 g

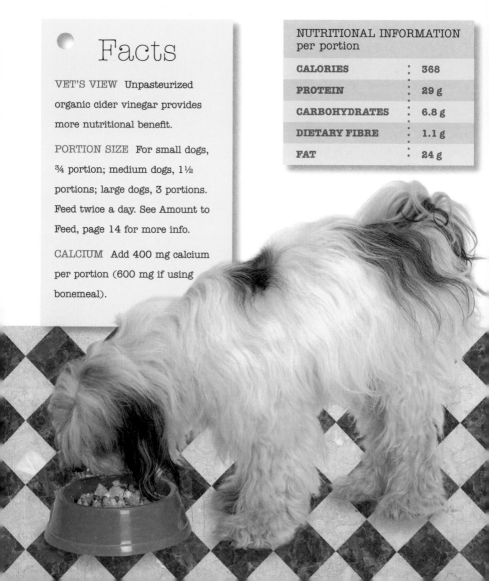

Recipe

Preparation Time: 15 minutes   Makes: 9 portions

- 🐾 **1.3 kg/3 lb skinless turkey pieces, light and dark meat**
- 🐾 **175 g/6 oz potato, diced**
- 🐾 **225 g/8 oz cottage cheese, 4% fat**
- 🐾 **125 g/4½ oz shelled fresh peas**
- 🐾 **1 tsp finely chopped garlic (see note on page 13)**
- 🐾 **2 tbsp cider vinegar**

1 Preheat oven to 180°C/350°F/Gas Mark 4. Oil a roasting tin. Roast the turkey (boneless breast or thigh, 30–45 minutes/boned breast or thigh, 45–60 minutes/whole turkey, 1½–2 hours) until the meat juices run clear when pierced with a skewer. Leave to cool.

2 Roast the potato with the turkey, or boil it until tender.

3 Remove the bones carefully and dice the meat into large pieces. Stir in the cider vinegar.

4 Mix together the turkey, cottage cheese, peas and potatoes.

5 Sprinkle the garlic over the top.

Sweet Chicken Dinner

The addition of pumpkin and black treacle will enhance the sheen of your dog's coat, plus dogs go crazy over black treacle – or look for blackstrap molasses in a health food shop.

Facts

VET'S VIEW For active dogs, increase the fat by leaving some of the skin on the chicken.

PORTION SIZE For small dogs, 1 portion; medium dogs, 2 portions; large dogs, 4 portions. Feed twice a day. See Amount to Feed on page 14.

CALCIUM Add 400 mg calcium per portion (600 mg if using bonemeal).

NUTRITIONAL INFORMATION
per portion

CALORIES	254
PROTEIN	30 g
CARBOHYDRATES	10 g
DIETARY FIBRE	0.6 g
FAT	9.6 g

Recipe

Preparation Time: 20 minutes   Makes: 9 portions

- 1.3 kg/3 lb skinless chicken, light and dark meat
- 225 g/8 oz fresh pumpkin purée
- 225 g/8 oz natural, full-fat yogurt
- 175 g/6 oz brown rice or barley
- 2 tbsp black treacle

1 Preheat oven to 180°C/350°F/Gas Mark 4 and lightly oil a roasting tin. Put the chicken in the roasting tin and roast (breast or thigh, 20–30 minutes/whole chicken, 45–60 minutes) until the meat juices run clear when pierced with a skewer. Leave to cool.

2 Remove all the bones and dice into large pieces.

3 Cook the rice or barley according to packet instructions.

4 Mix together the pumpkin, chicken and yogurt.

5 Put the rice or barley in the base of the feeding bowl, top with the chicken mixture and drizzle the treacle on top.

Morgan's Meal

Lamb is delicious but high in fat, so use sparingly for inactive dogs. Supplement with vitamin E when adding oils (see page 17).

Facts

VET'S VIEW Skin problems may benefit from fish oil, evening primrose oil or borage oil in place of olive oil in this recipe.

PORTION SIZE For small dogs, ½ portion; medium dogs, 1 portion; large dogs, 2 portions. Feed twice a day. See Amount to Feed on page 14.

CALCIUM Add 400 mg calcium per portion (600 mg if using bonemeal).

NUTRITIONAL INFORMATION
per portion

CALORIES	560
PROTEIN	46 g
CARBOHYDRATES	7.8 g
DIETARY FIBRE	1 g
FAT	37 g

Recipe

Preparation Time: 10 minutes   Makes: 5 portions

- 🐾 **1.3 kg/3 lb lamb mince or in chunks**
- 🐾 **2 tbsp black treacle**
- 🐾 **2 tsp olive oil**
- 🐾 **55 g/2 oz shelled peas**
- 🐾 **85 g/3 oz carrots, grated**

1 Fry the lamb over a medium heat for about 20 minutes until no longer pink and the meat juices run clear.

2 Mix the black treacle and olive oil into the meat. Leave to cool.

3 Once the lamb is cool, mix in the peas and carrots.

Minty Chicken

We love our dogs but not always their breath, so the addition of mint and parsley gives a natural breath freshener from the inside out.

NUTRITIONAL INFORMATION per portion	
CALORIES	239
PROTEIN	30 g
CARBOHYDRATES	6.9 g
DIETARY FIBRE	0.9 g
FAT	9.5 g

Facts

VET'S VIEW Bad breath can be a sign of dental disease, a broken tooth or even serious internal problems – always check with your vet when symptoms occur.

PORTION SIZE For small dogs, 1 portion; medium dogs, 2 portions; large dogs, 4 portions. Feed twice a day. See Amount to Feed on page 14.

CALCIUM Add 400 mg calcium per portion (600 mg if using bonemeal).

Recipe

Preparation Time: 20 minutes   Makes: 9 portions

- 🐾 1.3 kg/3 lb skinless chicken, light and dark meat
- 🐾 250 g/9 oz sweet potatoes, diced
- 🐾 225 g/8 oz natural full-fat yogurt
- 🐾 2 tbsp chopped fresh mint
- 🐾 2 tsp chopped fresh parsley

1 Preheat the oven to 180°C/350°F/Gas Mark 4. Lightly oil a roasting tin.

2 Roast the chicken (breast or thigh, 20–30 minutes/whole chicken, 45–60 minutes) until the meat juices run clear. Add the sweet potatoes for the final 25–30 minutes of cooking time. Leave to cool.

3 Remove all the bones and dice the meat into large pieces.

4 Peel the sweet potatoes and mix with the yogurt and herbs.

5 Mix together with the chicken.

Turkey Plate Special

This meal is a great way to please your pooch and freshen his breath at the same time. The apples and rice cleanse the palate, while the parsley naturally freshens it.

NUTRITIONAL INFORMATION per portion	
CALORIES	354
PROTEIN	27 g
CARBOHYDRATES	7.1 g
DIETARY FIBRE	0.8 g
FAT	24 g

Facts

VET'S VIEW Leave some turkey skin on for dogs that are active.

PORTION SIZE For small dogs, ¾ portion; medium dogs, 1½ portions; large dogs, 3 portions. Feed twice a day. See Amount to Feed, page 14.

CALCIUM Add 400 mg calcium per portion (600 mg if using bonemeal).

Recipe

Preparation Time: 15 minutes Makes: 8 portions

- 1.3 kg / 3 lb skinless turkey pieces, light and dark meat
- 2 tbsp chopped fresh parsley
- 2 tsp chopped fresh thyme
- 115 g / 4 oz cooked green beans, sliced
- 1 medium apple, diced
- 175 g / 6 oz brown rice

1 Preheat oven to 180°C/350°F/Gas Mark 4. Lightly oil a roasting tin. Roast the turkey (boneless breast or thigh, 30–45 minutes/boned breast or thigh, 45–60 minutes/whole turkey, 1½–2 hours) until the meat juices run clear. Leave to cool, remove all the bones and dice into large pieces.

2 Cook the rice according to packet instructions.

3 Mix the turkey with the parsley and thyme, and add the green beans, apple and rice.

Henny's Chicken Stew

This is a nice light dinner, good for hot days. The melon and mint freshen breath and aid your dog's digestion.

Facts

VET'S VIEW Mint and ginger can help relieve indigestion and nausea, but check with your vet before treating.

PORTION SIZE For small dogs, ⅞ portion; medium dogs, 1¾ portions; large dogs, 3½ portions. Feed twice a day. See Amount to Feed on page 14 for more info.

CALCIUM Add 400 mg calcium per portion (600 mg if using bonemeal).

NUTRITIONAL INFORMATION
per portion

CALORIES	286
PROTEIN	38 g
CARBOHYDRATES	8.3 g
DIETARY FIBRE	1.2 g
FAT	10 g

Recipe

Preparation Time: 15 minutes Makes: 9 portions

- 🐾 **1.3 kg/3 lb skinless chicken, light and dark meat**
- 🐾 **2 tbsp chopped fresh mint**
- 🐾 **225 g/8 oz canteloupe melon**
- 🐾 **200g/7 oz barley**
- 🐾 **55 g/2 oz shelled fresh peas**
- 🐾 **250 g/8 oz natural full-fat yogurt**

1. Preheat oven to 180°C/350°F/Gas Mark 4. Lightly oil a roasting tin.
2. Roast the chicken until the meat juices run clear. Leave to cool.
3. Remove all the bones and dice the meat into large pieces.
4. Cook the barley according to packet instructions.
5. Mix the mint with the melon.
6. Mix the chicken and peas with the barley, then add to the melon mix. Place a dollop of yogurt on top.

Chuckwagon Stew

This is a hearty meal fit for your furry friend, and non-gluten products are used to assist with some food allergies.

Facts

VET'S VIEW   Buffalo is lean, so it is suitable for dogs that cannot tolerate much fat. Virgin coconut oil can be added for calories.

PORTION SIZE   For small dogs, 1½ portions; medium dogs, 3 portions; large dogs, 6 portions. Feed twice a day. See Amount to Feed, page 14.

CALCIUM   Add 400 mg calcium per portion (600 mg if using bonemeal).

NUTRITIONAL INFORMATION
per portion

CALORIES	169
PROTEIN	27 g
CARBOHYDRATES	9.8 g
DIETARY FIBRE	1.6 g
FAT	1.8 g

Recipe

Preparation Time: 15 minutes   Makes: 10 portions

- 🐾 1.3 kg/3 lb buffalo mince or in chunks
- 🐾 250 g/9 oz sweet potatoes, diced
- 🐾 55 g/2 oz fresh peas, shelled
- 🐾 55 g/2 oz carrots, thinly sliced
- 🐾 55 g/2 oz cooked green beans, sliced
- 🐾 55 g/2 oz fresh spinach, torn (optional)
- 🐾 2 medium apples, diced

1 Fry the meat in a lightly sprayed pan over a medium heat for about 30 minutes until no longer pink, and the meat juices run clear. Leave to cool.
2 Bake the sweet potatoes at 180°C/350°F/Gas Mark 4 for 15 minutes until tender. Leave to cool, then peel and mash.
3 Mix the mash with the peas, carrots, beans and spinach.
4 Add the apples to the vegetable mixture.
5 Mix in the meat.

NOTES
Only serve dishes with spinach occasionally – the leaves have a high oxalate content, which can cause urinary crystals in dogs.

Scrumptious Delight

The addition of peaches gives the sweetness dogs enjoy, and non-gluten products are used to help with allergies.

Facts

VET'S VIEW Dogs prone to diarrhoea may have a gluten intolerance, so try this gluten-free recipe to see if it helps.

PORTION SIZE For small dogs, ⅝ portion; medium dogs, 1¼ portions; large dogs, 2½ portions. Feed twice a day. See Amount to Feed, page 14.

CALCIUM Add 400 mg calcium per portion (600 mg if using bonemeal).

NUTRITIONAL INFORMATION
per portion

CALORIES	446
PROTEIN	35 g
CARBOHYDRATES	12 g
DIETARY FIBRE	0.8 g
FAT	28 g

Recipe

Preparation Time: 10 minutes   Makes: 7 portions

- 🐾 **1.3 kg/3 lb lamb mince or in chunks**
- 🐾 **3 eggs**
- 🐾 **175 g/6 oz brown rice**
- 🐾 **55 g/2 oz fresh peas, shelled**
- 🐾 **225 g/8 oz tinned peach slices in natural juice**

1. Fry the meat in a lightly sprayed pan over a medium heat for about 15 minutes until no longer pink and the meat juices run clear. Leave to cool.
2. Meanwhile, cook the rice according to packet instructions.
3. Cook the eggs in a frying pan over a medium heat for about 5 minutes, stirring gently until the eggs are firm.
4. Mix the lamb with the scrambled eggs and leave to cool.
5. Mix together the peas, rice and peaches, then stir in the meat and egg mixture.

Spring Chicken Dinner

Dogs will go crazy over the tasty liver and root vegetables in this recipe.

Facts

VET'S VIEW Too much liver can cause loose stools, so reduce the amount if your dog has problems.

PORTION SIZE For small dogs, ¾ portion; medium dogs, 1½ portions; large dogs, 3 portions. Feed twice a day. See Amount to Feed on page 14 for more info.

CALCIUM Add 500 mg calcium per portion (800 mg if using bonemeal).

NUTRITIONAL INFORMATION per portion	
CALORIES	346
PROTEIN	48 g
CARBOHYDRATES	7.7 g
DIETARY FIBRE	1.5 g
FAT	12 g

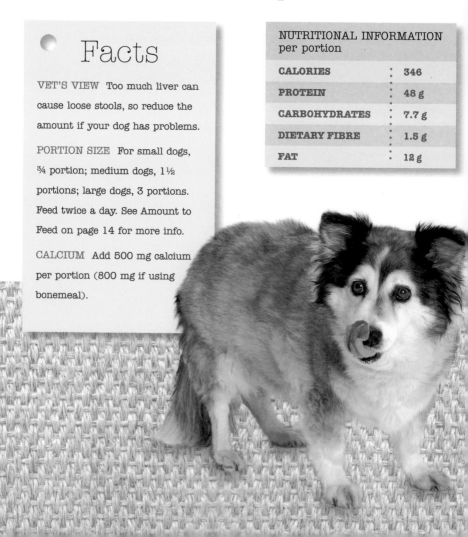

Recipe

Preparation Time: 25 minutes Makes: 8 portions

- 🐾 **1.3 kg/3 lb skinless chicken**
- 🐾 **1–2 medium yams or sweet potatoes**
- 🐾 **225 g/8 oz chicken livers**
- 🐾 **115 g/4 oz fresh peas, shelled**

1 Preheat oven to 180°C/350°F/Gas Mark 4.
2 Lightly oil a roasting tin. Roast the chicken (breast or thigh, 20–30 minutes/whole chicken, 45–60 minutes) until the meat juices run clear. Add the yams or sweet potatoes for the final 25–30 minutes of the cooking time. Leave to cool. Peel and dice.
3 Remove all bones and dice the meat into large pieces.
4 Put the livers in a saucepan with just enough water to cover. Simmer until the livers become firm. Leave to cool.
5 Dice the livers and mix with the chicken, yams/potatoes and peas.

Feeling Blue Diet

This is a great replacement meal for when your pup is under the weather, but always check with a vet if your dog seems too blue.

Facts

VET'S VIEW Overcooked rice with extra water ('rice congee') helps soothe digestive upset.

PORTION SIZE For small dogs, ¾ portion; medium dogs, 1½ portions; large dogs, 3 portions. Feed twice a day. See Amount to Feed, page 14.

CALCIUM Add 400 mg calcium per portion (600 mg if using bonemeal).

NUTRITIONAL INFORMATION
per portion

CALORIES	337
PROTEIN	42 g
CARBOHYDRATES	14 g
DIETARY FIBRE	0.4 g
FAT	11 g

Recipe

Preparation Time: 15 minutes   Makes: 11 portions

- 🐾 **1.8 kg / 4 lb extra lean beef mince or skinless chicken**
- 🐾 **350 g / 12 oz brown rice**
- 🐾 **250 g / 9 oz apple sauce**

1 Simmer the meat in a saucepan in enough water to cover for about 15 minutes until the meat is no longer pink. Drain from water. Leave to cool.

2 Cook the rice for 15 minutes longer than it says on the packet.

3 Shred the chicken or pulverize the beef into very small pieces.

4 Thoroughly mix the rice and apple sauce into the meat.

NOTES

Dogs with diarrhoea should be fed bland low-fat meals. If using beef, boil and remove all fat, or rinse after cooking to remove fat.

Natural Laxative Diet

A natural remedy to relieve extra-firm stools.

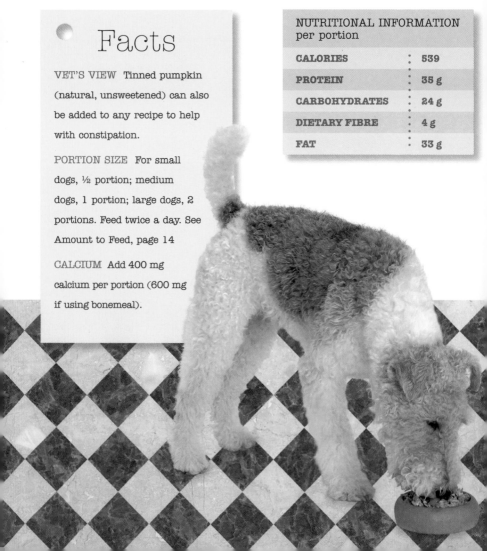

Facts

VET'S VIEW Tinned pumpkin (natural, unsweetened) can also be added to any recipe to help with constipation.

PORTION SIZE For small dogs, ½ portion; medium dogs, 1 portion; large dogs, 2 portions. Feed twice a day. See Amount to Feed, page 14

CALCIUM Add 400 mg calcium per portion (600 mg if using bonemeal).

NUTRITIONAL INFORMATION per portion	
CALORIES	539
PROTEIN	35 g
CARBOHYDRATES	24 g
DIETARY FIBRE	4 g
FAT	33 g

Recipe

Preparation Time: 20 minutes   Makes: 7 portions

- 🐾 **1.3 kg/3 lb lean beef mince or in chunks**
- 🐾 **2 prunes**
- 🐾 **200 g/7 oz barley**
- 🐾 **175 g/6 oz porridge oats**
- 🐾 **225 g/8 oz natural full-fat yogurt**

1 Simmer the meat in a saucepan with enough water to cover for about 15 minutes until it is no longer pink and the juices run clear. Drain and leave to cool.

2 Cook the barley and oats according to packet instructions.

3 Pulverize the beef into small pieces (unless using beef mince).

4 Dice the prunes.

5 Thoroughly mix all the ingredients together.

Resources

The internet provides a wealth of resources – here is a selection.

www.onlynaturalpet.com/ holistic-healthcare-library/ allergies/109/the-role-of- protein-in-good-nutrition.aspx
Discusses the importance of diet when dealing with allergies in dogs.

www.dogfoodadvisor.com/dog- feeding-tips/dog-lose-weight/
Talks about how home-made diets can help dogs lose weight.

www.balanceit.com
www.cookforyourdog.com
Companies who make vitamin-mineral mixes designed to balance out home-made diets, including calcium.

www.caberfeidh.com/HHC.htm
Holistic health care, including information on home-made diets, natural flea control and more.

www.dogaware.com
Information on home-made diets, including diet and supplements for a variety of health issues.

www.mycockerspaniel.com/ mer.htm
This website provides calorie recommendations for dogs.

www.petdietdesigner.com
Nutritional analysis tools.

Index

Acknowledgements

The publishers would like to thank the following dogs and their owners for their participation in this book.

Sumo the Boxer (Sue Warde)

Ellie the Golden Retriever (Andrew & Janette Lawes)

Woody the Fox Terrier (Kevin & Pat Knight)

Holly the Husky Mix (Kathy Laird)

Mukha & Samadhi the Tibetan Terriers (Tula Dyer)

Ted the Patterdale Terrier (Sophie Collins)